Meet the Artist™

Edgar Dugas

Melody S. Mis

PowerKiDS
press.

New York

To the Raben and Bonnell children, who make life so much fun

Published in 2008 by The Rosen Publishing Group, Inc.
29 East 21st Street, New York, NY 10010

First Edition

Editor: Jennifer Way
Book Design: Greg Tucker
Photo Researcher: Nicole Pristash

3 9082 10639 3732

Photo Credits: All background images by Shutterstock; cover © Giraudon, Musée d'Orsay, Paris, France/The Bridgeman Art Library International; p. 5 © Giraudon, Museu Calouste Gulbenkian, Lisbon, Portugal/The Bridgeman Art Library International; p. 7 (top) © Giraudon, Musée d'Orsay, Paris, France/The Bridgeman Art Library International; pp. 7 (bottom), 11 (bottom) by Shutterstock; p. 9 © Fogg Art Museum, Bequest of Grenville L. Winthrop, Harvard University Art Museums/The Bridgeman Art Library International; p. 11 © Birmingham Museums and Art Gallery/The Bridgeman Art Library International; p. 13 © Lauros/Giraudon, Musée d'Orsay, Paris, France/The Bridgeman Art Library International; p. 14 © Pushkin Museum, Moscow, Russia/The Bridgeman Art Library International; p. 16 © Metropolitan Museum of Art, New York/The Bridgeman Art Library International; p. 18 © Giraudon, Musée d'Orsay, Paris, France/The Bridgeman Art Library International; p. 21 © Photo © Christie's Images, Private Collection/The Bridgeman Art Library International.

Library of Congress Cataloging-in-Publication Data

Mis, Melody S.
  Edgar Degas / Melody S. Mis. — 1st ed.
    p. cm. — (Meet the artist)
  Includes index.
  ISBN-13: 978-1-4042-3839-8 (library binding)
  ISBN-10: 1-4042-3839-5 (library binding)
  1. Degas, Edgar, 1834–1917—Juvenile literature. 2. Painters—France—Biography—Juvenile literature. I. Title.
  ND553.D3M57 2008
  709.2—dc22
  [B]

                          2007006498

Manufactured in the United States of America

CONTENTS

Meet Edgar Degas

Edgar Degas was a French artist. He is famous for his paintings, drawings, and **sculptures** of **ballet** dancers. Degas is known as one of the leaders of impressionism. Impressionist artists painted common everyday scenes. They also liked to paint outdoors so they could copy the bright colors of nature.

Like the impressionists, Degas painted scenes of modern life, but he did not paint outdoors. Instead, he learned a scene by heart and painted it in his **studio**.

Degas became a famous and well-loved artist during his lifetime. He **influenced** other important artists, such as America's Mary Cassatt.

This is a self-portrait Degas made in 1862, when he was 28. A self-portrait is a painting done by the artist of himself or herself.

Young Degas

Edgar Degas was born in Paris, France, in 1834. He was the oldest of five children. Degas' family was fairly well off. His mother, Celestine, died when he was 13 years old. His father, Auguste, was interested in art and often took young Edgar to the Louvre, the largest art **museum** in Paris.

At age 11, Degas went to high school, where he first studied drawing. After he finished high school, in 1853, Degas entered law school. Instead of studying law, however, Degas went to the Louvre and copied famous paintings. After a few months, Degas left law school to study art.

Top: Degas painted many portraits of family members. He did this portrait of his grandfather Hilaire Degas in 1857.

Bottom: The Louvre is one of the oldest and most famous art museums in the world.

Studying Art

Degas studied painting for several months in 1854 at Paris's School of Fine Arts. He also took art lessons from Louis Lamothe. Lamothe **encouraged** Degas to copy the paintings of the old masters. The old masters are famous artists who painted between about 1400 and 1800. They made paintings of people and events from history, **religion**, and **mythology**. The old masters were known for their use of light and **perspective** to make realistic paintings.

In 1855, Degas met the French painter Jean-Auguste-Dominique Ingres. Ingres believed drawing skills were important in painting. He told Degas to practice drawing, which Degas did for the rest of his life.

Jean-Auguste-Dominique Ingres, shown here in a self-portrait, was one of the most respected French painters of his time. Louis Lamothe had studied with Ingres. He passed on Ingres' way of painting to Degas.

Degas Goes to Italy

In 1856, Degas went to Italy to study the great paintings of Italy's old masters. These paintings were displayed, or shown, in Italy's museums and churches. He also wanted to get to know his aunts and uncles who lived in Italy.

While Degas was in Italy, he painted his aunt Laura Bellelli's family. He also drew pictures of Italy's famous monuments. Degas joined a group of young Italian artists who were **experimenting** with new ideas. Instead of painting people or events from the past, these artists were painting scenes they saw every day.

Top: A Roman Beggar Woman is an example of the paintings with everyday subjects that Degas painted while he was in Italy.

Bottom: Degas studied the old masters at places like the Vatican Museums, near Rome, Italy.

11

The French Impressionists

Degas returned to Paris in 1859. In 1862, he became friends with an impressionist artist named Édouard Manet. Manet encouraged Degas to send his paintings to the Paris Salon, the city's largest art **exhibition**. Manet thought it would help Degas' **career** if people saw his paintings there. Several of Degas' paintings were shown at the salon from 1865 to 1870.

Manet told Degas to stop copying the old masters. He encouraged Degas to paint scenes from theaters and other places he saw in everyday life. Degas began to paint the world around him. Some of his favorite things to paint were horse races and ballet dancers.

The Parade, or *Race Horses in Front of the Stands*, is one of the many paintings Degas made of horse racing. This sport was well liked in France at that time but had not been shown in paintings until Degas'.

Above: Blue Dancers is one of Degas' later pictures of dancers.

Pages 16–17: Degas often made several paintings that were very much alike. There are two other paintings that are very much like this one, *The Rehearsal of the Ballet on Stage.*

Degas' Dancers

In 1871, Degas began to study ballet dancers while they danced and rested. He was interested in their movements and their colorful costumes. He wanted to **capture** their actions while they tied their shoes, fixed their costumes, and danced. Degas also began to experiment with the effect light had on the colors of the dancers' costumes.

Degas' paintings of dancers became so popular that he had a hard time painting enough of them to sell. During his life, Degas made about 1,500 paintings and drawings of dancers!

Degas painted *In a Café*, or *The Absinthe*, in 1876. This famous painting was made during the time he was showing his work in the impressionist exhibitions.

The Impressionists' Exhibitions

During the time that Degas lived, the Paris Salon displayed only paintings done in established styles. Since the impressionists painted modern scenes of everyday life, the salon did not want to show their paintings. This meant that the impressionists had to find another way to show their works. Starting in 1874, Degas and a group of impressionist artists planned eight exhibitions that were held in Paris between 1874 and 1886.

The impressionists' exhibitions gave artists a place where they could display and sell their paintings. Degas entered his paintings of women working and women bathing at these shows. Some people liked these paintings. Others thought his paintings were terrible.

The Little Dancer

In the 1880s, Degas began to have problems with his sight. He tried doing different kinds of art in the hope that they would be easier on his eyes. He started to use pastels instead of oil paints. Pastels are bright-colored sticks that are something like crayons. Using pastels, Degas could draw and color his subjects at the same time.

Degas also began to make sculptures of horses and dancers out of wax. His most famous sculpture is called *The Little Dancer*. After Degas had shaped the wax body of the dancer, he put real clothes and hair on her. Many people were shocked when they saw the dressed sculpture.

You can see that *The Little Dancer* sculpture is still wearing the same clothes that were put on her when she was created! Seeing a sculpture wearing clothes was considered shocking when Degas did it in 1881.

Degas in Later Years

Degas was known for having a few strange habits. He liked to buy paintings by other artists, but he did not like to sell his own paintings. After his father died, in 1874, Degas was left with a lot of his father's unpaid bills. Degas was then forced to sell his own paintings and the paintings he had bought to help pay these bills.

Degas never married. He did not believe that an artist had enough time for both work and a family. Degas spent much of his later life alone. He died on September 27, 1917, at the age of 83.

GLOSSARY

ballet (BA-lay) A type of dance that uses graceful movements and often tells a story.

capture (KAP-chur) To keep.

career (kuh-REER) The work a person chooses to do.

encouraged (in-KUR-ijd) Gave someone reason to do something.

exhibition (ek-suh-BIH-shun) A public show.

experimenting (ik-SPER-uh-ment-ing) Trying something new or different.

influenced (IN-floo-entsd) Got others to do something.

museum (myoo-ZEE-um) A place where art or historical pieces are safely kept for people to see and to study.

mythology (mih-THAH-luh-jee) A body of stories that people make up to explain things.

perspective (per-SPEK-tiv) Point of view. Perspective helps make a painting look real.

religion (rih-LIH-jen) A belief in and a way of honoring a god or gods.

sculptures (SKULP-cherz) Figures that are shaped or formed.

studio (STOO-dee-oh) A room or building where an artist works.

INDEX

WEB SITES

Due to the changing nature of Internet links, PowerKids
Press has developed an online list of Web sites related to the subject of
this book. This site is updated regularly. Please use this link to access the list:
www.powerkidslinks.com/mta/degas/